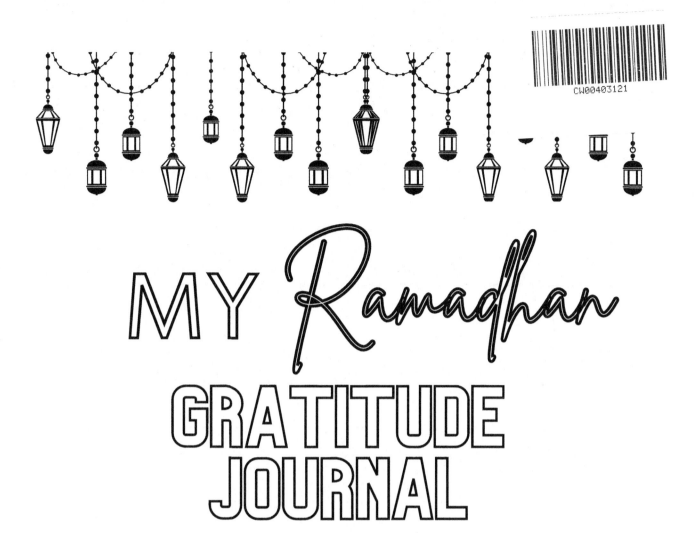

MY Ramadhan
GRATITUDE JOURNAL

Belongs to:

_____

_____

Ramadhan Mubarak

Countdown to Eid!

1	2	3	4	5
6	7	8	9	10
11	12	13	14	15
16	17	18	19	20
21	22	23	24	25
26	27	28	29	30

Khatmul Quran IN 30 DAYS

Samurah bin Jundub narrated that the Messenger of Allah said, "There are 4 words dearest to Allah: 'Subhanallah (Glory be to Allah)', 'Alhamdulillah (Praise be to Allah)', 'Laa ilaaha illallah (There is no God but Allah)', and 'Allahuakbar (God is Most Great)'. It does not matter which you say first."
(Muslim)

JUZ	SURAH	DATE	COMPLETED
1	AL FATIHAH 1 - AL BAQARAH 141		
2	AL BAQARAH 142 - AL BAQARAH 252		
3	AL BAQARAH 253 - AL IMRAN 92		
4	AL IMRAN 93 - AN NISAA 23		
5	AN NISAA 24 - AN NISAA 147		
6	AN NISAA 148 - AL MA'IDAH 81		
7	AL MA'IDAH 82 - AL AN'AM 110		
8	AL AN'AM 111 - AL A'RAF 87		
9	AL A'RAF 88 - AL ANFAL 40		
10	AL ANFAL 41 - AT TAUBA 92		
11	AT TAUBA 93 - HUD 5		
12	HUD 6 - YUSUF 52		
13	YUSUF 53 - IBRAHIM 52		
14	AL HIJR 1 - AN NAHL 128		
15	AL ISRA' 1 - AL KAHF 74		
16	AL KAHF 75 - TA HA 135		
17	AL ANBIYA' 1 - AL HAJJ 78		
18	AL MU'MINUN 1 - AL FURQAN 20		
19	AL FURQAN 21 - AN NAML 55		
20	AN NAML 56 - AL ANKABUT 45		
21	AL ANKABUT 46 - AL AHZAB 30		
22	AL AHZAB 31 - YASIN 27		
23	YASIN 28 - AZ ZUMAR 31		
24	AZ ZUMAR 32 - FUSSILAT 46		
25	FUSSILAT 47 - AL JATHIYAH 37		
26	AL AHQAF 1 - ADH DHARIYAT 30		
27	ADH DHARIYAT 31 - AL HADID 29		
28	AL MUJADILAH 1 - AT TAHRIM 12		
29	AL MULK 1 - AL MURSALAT 50		
30	AN NABA' 1 - AN NAS 6		

Ramadhan
DAY 1

DAY ☐ **DATE/YEAR**
M/T/W/T/F/S/S

☐

MEAL PLAN

SUHOOR:

IFTAR:

Prayers

SALAT		ON TIME
Maghrib	Sunnah	☐
Isha	Sunnah	☐
Fajr	Sunnah	☐
Dhuhr	Sunnah	☐
Asr	Sunnah	☐
Taraweeh		
Qiyam		

Hadeeth of The Day

Hadhrat Abu Hurairah in a lengthy hadith, narrates that The Prophet Muhammad PBUH said:
"I swear by That Being in Whose possession is the life of The Prophet Muhammad! The odour of the mouth of a fasting person is sweeter to Allah Ta'ala than the fragrance of musk."
(Bukhari)

I am *Grateful* for...

_____
_____

GOALS

Act of Kindness

Smile!	Make Dua
Sadaqah	Spend Time with Family
Read Qur'an	Be Helpful

Healthy Habits

WATER:

EXERCISE: _ _ _ _ _ _ _ _ _ _ _

MOOD:

Qur'an TRACKER

VERSE: ☐ **SURAH:** ☐ **JUZ':** ☐

Ramadhan DAY 2

DAY ☐
DATE/YEAR
M/T/W/T/F/S/S

MEAL PLAN
SUHOOR:
IFTAR:

Prayers

SALAT		ON TIME
Maghrib	Sunnah	☐
Isha	Sunnah	☐
Fajr	Sunnah	☐
Dhuhr	Sunnah	☐
Asr	Sunnah	☐
Taraweeh		
Qiyam		

Hadeeth of the Day

Hadhrat Abu 'Ubaidah reports: "I have heard Rasulullah PBUH saying: "Fasting is protective covering for a man as long as he does not tear that protection."
(Nasai, Ibn Majah and Ibn Khuzaimah)

I am Grateful for...
_____
_____

GOALS

Act of Kindness

Smile!	Make Dua
Sadaqah	Spend Time with Family
Read Qur'an	Be Helpful

Healthy Habits

WATER:

EXERCISE: _ _ _ _ _ _ _ _ _ _

MOOD: 😀 😴 😢 😠

Qur'an TRACKER

VERSE: ☐   SURAH: ☐   JUZ': ☐

Reflections

Ramadhan
DAY 3

MEAL PLAN

SUHOOR:

IFTAR:

---

prayers

SALAT		ON TIME
Maghrib	Sunnah	☐
Isha	Sunnah	☐
Fajr	Sunnah	☐
Dhuhr	Sunnah	☐
Asr	Sunnah	☐
Taraweeh		
Qiyam		

Hadeeth of The Day

Hadhrat Abu Hurairah narrates that The Prophet Muhammad PBUH said:
"Whosoever eats on one day of Ramadhan without a valid reason or excuse or genuine illness (acceptable in Shari-'ah), shall never be able to compensate for that day even by fasting the rest of his life."
(Ahmad, Tirmizhi, Abu Dawood and Ibn Majah)

I am *Grateful* for...
_____
_____
_____

GOALS

Act of Kindness

Smile!	Make Dua
Sadaqah	Spend Time with Family
Read Qur'an	Be Helpful

Healthy Habits

WATER:

EXERCISE: _ _ _ _ _ _ _ _ _ _ _

MOOD: 😀 😴 🙁 😠

Qur'an TRACKER

VERSE: _____   SURAH: _____   JUZ': _____

DAY ☐ **DATE/YEAR** M/T/W/T/F/S/S

MEAL PLAN

SUHOOR:

IFTAR:

Prayers

SALAT		ON TIME
Maghrib	Sunnah	☐
Isha	Sunnah	☐
Fajr	Sunnah	☐
Dhuhr	Sunnah	☐
Asr	Sunnah	☐
Taraweeh		
Qiyam		

Hadeeth of The Day

Hadhrat Abu Hurairah narrates that The Prophet Muhammad PBUH said: "Keep fasting and you will remain healthy."

(Tibrani)

I am *Grateful* for...
_____
_____

GOALS

Act of Kindness

Smile!	Make Dua
Sadaqah	Spend Time with Family
Read Qur'an	Be Helpful

Healthy Habits

WATER:

EXERCISE: _ _ _ _ _ _ _ _ _

MOOD:

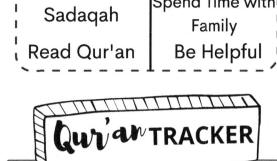

VERSE: | **SURAH:** | **JUZ':**

Reflections

Ramadhan
DAY 5

DAY ☐

DATE/YEAR
M/T/W/T/F/S/S

MEAL PLAN

SUHOOR:

IFTAR:

---

prayers

SALAT		ON TIME
Maghrib	Sunnah	☐
Isha	Sunnah	☐
Fajr	Sunnah	☐
Dhuhr	Sunnah	☐
Asr	Sunnah	☐
Taraweeh		
Qiyam		

Hadeeth of the Day

Hadhrat Ibn Umar narrates, in a lengthy hadith, that The Prophet Muhammad PBUH said:
"Fasting is exclusively for Allah Ta'ala. The thawaab (reward) of it (being limitless) no one knows besides Allah Ta'ala."

(Tabrani, Baihaqi)

I am Grateful for...
_____
_____

GOALS

Act of Kindness

Smile!	Make Dua
Sadaqah	Spend Time with Family
Read Qur'an	Be Helpful

Healthy Habits

WATER:

EXERCISE: _ _ _ _ _ _ _ _ _ _ _

MOOD:

Qur'an TRACKER

VERSE: | SURAH: | JUZ':

Ramadhan DAY 6

DAY ☐

DATE/YEAR
M/T/W/T/F/S/S

MEAL PLAN

SUHOOR: _____

IFTAR: _____

Prayers

SALAT		ON TIME
Maghrib	Sunnah	☐
Isha	Sunnah	☐
Fajr	Sunnah	☐
Dhuhr	Sunnah	☐
Asr	Sunnah	☐
Taraweeh		
Qiyam		

Hadeeth of The Day

Hadhrat Mu'adz Ibn Jabal narrates: I heard The Prophet Muhammad PBUH saying:
"He who meets Allah in such a state that he does not ascribe any partner to Him, observes the five times Salat and fasts during the month of Ramadhan, he will be forgiven."

(Musnad Ahmad)

I am *Grateful* for...
_____
_____

GOALS

Act of Kindness

Smile!	Make Dua
Sadaqah	Spend Time with Family
Read Qur'an	Be Helpful

Healthy Habits

WATER: ☐☐☐☐☐☐☐☐

EXERCISE: _____

MOOD: 😀 😴 ☹️ 😠

Qur'an TRACKER

VERSE: ☐ SURAH: ☐ JUZ': ☐

Reflections

Ramadhan
DAY 7

DAY ☐ **DATE/YEAR**
M/T/W/T/F/S/S ☐

MEAL PLAN

SUHOOR: ☐

IFTAR: ☐

Prayers

SALAT		ON TIME
Maghrib	Sunnah	☐
Isha	Sunnah	☐
Fajr	Sunnah	☐
Dhuhr	Sunnah	☐
Asr	Sunnah	☐
Taraweeh		
Qiyam		

Hadeeth of The Day

Hadhrat Abu Hurairah narrates that The Prophet Muhammad PBUH said:
"The best month for fasting after the month of Ramadhan, is the month of Al-Muharram, and the best Salat after obligatory Salat, is Tahajjud Salat."
(Muslim)

I am *Grateful* for...
_____
_____

GOALS

Act of Kindness

Smile!	Make Dua
Sadaqah	Spend Time with Family
Read Qur'an	Be Helpful

Healthy Habits

WATER: ☐ ☐ ☐ ☐ ☐ ☐ ☐ ☐

EXERCISE: _ _ _ _ _ _ _ _ _ _

MOOD: 😀 😴 😢 😠

Qur'an TRACKER

VERSE: [ ] SURAH: [ ] JUZ': [ ]

Reflections

Ramadhan
DAY 8

DAY ☐ **DATE/YEAR**
M/T/W/T/F/S/S

MEAL PLAN

SUHOOR:

IFTAR:

Prayers

SALAT		ON TIME
Maghrib	Sunnah	☐
Isha	Sunnah	☐
Fajr	Sunnah	☐
Dhuhr	Sunnah	☐
Asr	Sunnah	☐
Taraweeh		
Qiyam		

Hadeeth of The Day

Hadhrat Abu Sa'id Al – Khudri narrates that The Prophet Muhammad PBUH said: "He who fasts for a day in the Path of Allah, Allah will keep him away from Hell by a distance of seventy years of journey."

(Nasai)

I am *Grateful* for...

_____
_____

GOALS

Act of Kindness

Smile!	Make Dua
Sadaqah	Spend Time with Family
Read Qur'an	Be Helpful

Healthy Habits

WATER:

EXERCISE: _ _ _ _ _ _ _ _ _ _ _

MOOD:

Qur'an TRACKER

VERSE: ____ SURAH: ____ JUZ': ____

Reflections

DAY ☐

DATE/YEAR
M/T/W/T/F/S/S

MEAL PLAN

SUHOOR:

IFTAR:

Prayers

SALAT		ON TIME
Maghrib	Sunnah	☐
Isha	Sunnah	☐
Fajr	Sunnah	☐
Dhuhr	Sunnah	☐
Asr	Sunnah	☐
Taraweeh		
Qiyam		

Hadeeth of The Day

Hadhrat Abu Umamah Bahiliy narrates that The Prophet Muhammad PBUH said: "If anyone fasts for a day in the Path of Allah, Allah puts a trench between him and Hell, which is as wide as the distance between the heavens and the earth."

(Tirmizhi)

I am *Grateful* for...

_____
_____

GOALS

Act of Kindness

Smile!	Make Dua
Sadaqah	Spend Time with Family
Read Qur'an	Be Helpful

Healthy Habits

WATER:

EXERCISE: _ _ _ _ _ _ _ _ _ _ _

MOOD:

Qur'an TRACKER

VERSE: ☐   SURAH: ☐   JUZ': ☐

Reflections

Explanation of Maulana Thanwi

Maulana Thanwi says, "If Allah announces at the end of Ramadhan that my servants have understood the reality of Ramadhan and they are making Dua for the entire year must be Ramadhan, so let Me make it 10 days more. Throughout the night, they will be thinking that they will have to sit for another 10 days. Allah knows our temperaments, He knows us better then we know ourselves.

He mentions in the Qur'an:

هُوَأَعْلَمُ بِكُمْ إِذْأَنْشَأَكُمْ مِّنَ الْأَرْ
ضِ وَإِذْ أَنتُمْ أَجِنَّةٌ فِبُطُونَ أُمَّهَاتِكُمْ فَلَا تُزَكُّوٓاأَنفُسَكُم
هو أَاعلم بِ ن اتَّقى

He was best aware of you when He created you from the earth and when you were fetuses in the wombs of your mothers. So do not ascribe purity (piety) to yourselves. He knows best who is the most pious (whose level of Taqwa is highest).

Never try to act pious and holy before Allah as He knows you perfectly well. Outwardly we may show people that we are very pious and very holy but Allah says, "I know you perfectly well."

Enjoyment is in Profits

The fast of Ramadhan may be strenuous on a person but it is definitely enjoyable as he knows of the profit that he is going to accumulate. This is similar to the month of December for a businessman. It may be strenuous on him but he looks forward to December as he will be making more money than usual.

Another example to understand this point, a husband and wife get married and on the first night the husband tells the wife, "I've been preparing for our wedding, for the past 6 months, for the last 6 weeks I was trying to get the house ready, preparing our home, room, getting the furniture, etc." I used to sleep after twelve and awaken for work the next morning. The wife replies, "I also worked very hard. Yesterday, I went to get my hair done. After doing my hair, I hardly slept because I had to sit on the chair throughout the night so I don't spoil my hair. Now, let's have a good night sleep and we will see to other things later.

All the tiredness disappear on the first night!

DAY ☐ **DATE/YEAR**
M/T/W/T/F/S/S

MEAL PLAN
SUHOOR: ☐
IFTAR: ☐

Prayers

SALAT		ON TIME
Maghrib	Sunnah	☐
Isha	Sunnah	☐
Fajr	Sunnah	☐
Dhuhr	Sunnah	☐
Asr	Sunnah	☐
Taraweeh		
Qiyam		

Hadeeth of the Day

Hadhrat Abu Hurairah reported The Prophet PBUH saying:
"The time between the five prayers, two consecutive Friday prayers, and two consecutive Ramadhans are expiations for all that has happened during that period, provided that one has avoided the grave sins."

(Muslim)

I am Grateful for...
_____
_____

GOALS

Act of Kindness

Smile!	Make Dua
Sadaqah	Spend Time with Family
Read Qur'an	Be Helpful

Healthy Habits

WATER: ☐☐☐☐☐☐☐☐

EXERCISE: _ _ _ _ _ _ _ _ _ _ _

MOOD: 😃 😴 😢 😠

Qur'an Tracker

VERSE: ☐ SURAH: ☐ JUZ': ☐

Reflections

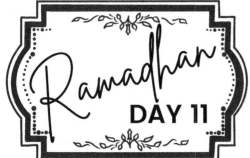

Ramadhan
DAY 11

DAY ☐ **DATE/YEAR**
M/T/W/T/F/S/S [   ]

MEAL PLAN

SUHOOR:

IFTAR:

Prayers

SALAT		ON TIME
Maghrib	Sunnah	☐
Isha	Sunnah	☐
Fajr	Sunnah	☐
Dhuhr	Sunnah	☐
Asr	Sunnah	☐
Taraweeh		
Qiyam		

Hadeeth of The Day

Abu Sa'id al-Khudri narrated that The Prophet PBUH said:
"Whoever fasts the month of Ramadhan, obeying all of its limitations and guarding himself against what is forbidden, has in fact atoned for any sins he committed before it."
(Ahmad and Al-Baihaqi)

I am Grateful for...
_____
_____

GOALS

Act of Kindness

Smile!	Make Dua
Sadaqah	Spend Time with Family
Read Qur'an	Be Helpful

Healthy Habits

WATER:

EXERCISE: _____

MOOD: 😀 😴 🙁 😠

Qur'an TRACKER

VERSE: [   ]   **SURAH:** [   ]   **JUZ':** [   ]

Reflections

Ramadhan DAY 12

DAY ☐ **DATE/YEAR M/T/W/T/F/S/S** ☐

MEAL PLAN

SUHOOR:

IFTAR:

Prayers

SALAT		ON TIME
Maghrib	Sunnah	☐
Isha	Sunnah	☐
Fajr	Sunnah	☐
Dhuhr	Sunnah	☐
Asr	Sunnah	☐
Taraweeh		
Qiyam		

Hadeeth of The Day

Hadhrat 'Aishah said:
"I never saw the Messenger of Allah fast a complete month save for Ramadhan, and I have never seen him fast more in a month than he did in Sha'ban."

(Bukhari and Muslim)

I am *Grateful* for...

_____
_____

GOALS

Act of Kindness

Smile!	Make Dua
Sadaqah	Spend Time with Family
Read Qur'an	Be Helpful

Healthy Habits

WATER:

EXERCISE: _ _ _ _ _ _ _ _ _

MOOD:

Qur'an TRACKER

VERSE: [   ]   SURAH: [   ]   JUZ': [   ]

Reflections

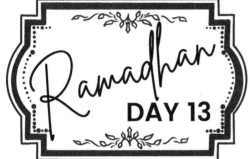

Ramadhan
DAY 13

DAY ☐ **DATE/YEAR** M/T/W/T/F/S/S

MEAL PLAN

SUHOOR:

IFTAR:

Prayers

SALAT		ON TIME
Maghrib	Sunnah	☐
Isha	Sunnah	☐
Fajr	Sunnah	☐
Dhuhr	Sunnah	☐
Asr	Sunnah	☐
Taraweeh		
Qiyam		

Hadeeth of The Day

Hadhrat Anas reported that the Messenger of Allah PBUH said:
"Eat a pre-dawn meal (sahur or sahri), for there are blessings in it."

(Bukhari and Muslim)

I am *Grateful* for...
_____
_____

GOALS

Act of Kindness

Smile!	Make Dua
Sadaqah	Spend Time with Family
Read Qur'an	Be Helpful

Healthy Habits

WATER:

EXERCISE: _ _ _ _ _ _ _ _ _ _

MOOD: 😀 😴 🙁 😠

Qur'an TRACKER

VERSE: [ ] SURAH: [ ] JUZ': [ ]

Reflections

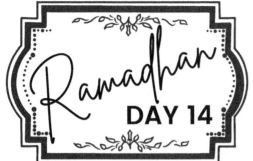

Ramadhan
DAY 14

DAY ☐ **DATE/YEAR** M/T/W/T/F/S/S ☐

MEAL PLAN
SUHOOR:

IFTAR:

Prayers

SALAT		ON TIME
Maghrib	Sunnah	☐
Isha	Sunnah	☐
Fajr	Sunnah	☐
Dhuhr	Sunnah	☐
Asr	Sunnah	☐
Taraweeh		
Qiyam		

Hadeeth of The Day

Hadhrat Abu Sa'id al-Khudri reported that The Prophet Muhammad PBUH said:
"The pre-dawn meal is blessed, so do not neglect it even if you only take a sip of water. Verily, Allah and the angels pray for those who have pre-dawn meals."
(Ahmad)

I am *Grateful* for...
_____
_____

GOALS

Act of Kindness

Smile!	Make Dua
Sadaqah	Spend Time with Family
Read Qur'an	Be Helpful

Healthy Habits

WATER: ☐☐☐☐☐☐☐☐

EXERCISE: _ _ _ _ _ _ _ _

MOOD: 😀 😴 ☹️ 😠

Qur'an TRACKER

VERSE: ☐   **SURAH:** ☐   **JUZ':** ☐

Reflections

Ramadhan
DAY 15

DAY ☐

DATE/YEAR
M/T/W/T/F/S/S

MEAL PLAN

SUHOOR:

IFTAR:

prayers

SALAT		ON TIME
Maghrib	Sunnah	☐
Isha	Sunnah	☐
Fajr	Sunnah	☐
Dhuhr	Sunnah	☐
Asr	Sunnah	☐
Taraweeh		
Qiyam		

Hadeeth of The Day

Hadhrat Sahl Ibn Sa'ad reported that the Prophet PBUH said:
"The people will always be with the good as long as they hasten in breaking the fast."

(Bukhari and Muslim)

I am Grateful for...

_____
_____

GOALS

Act of Kindness

Smile!	Make Dua
Sadaqah	Spend Time with Family
Read Qur'an	Be Helpful

Healthy Habits

WATER:

EXERCISE: _ _ _ _ _ _ _ _ _ _ _ _

MOOD:

Qur'an TRACKER

VERSE: [   ]   SURAH: [   ]   JUZ': [   ]

Reflections

Ramadhan
DAY 16

DAY ☐ **DATE/YEAR** M/T/W/T/F/S/S ☐

MEAL PLAN
- SUHOOR:
- IFTAR:

Prayers

SALAT		ON TIME
Maghrib	Sunnah	☐
Isha	Sunnah	☐
Fajr	Sunnah	☐
Dhuhr	Sunnah	☐
Asr	Sunnah	☐
Taraweeh		
Qiyam		

Hadeeth of the Day

Hadhrat Abu Ayyub al-Ansari reported Allah's Messenger PBUH as saying:
"He who observed the fast of Ramadhan and then followed it with six (fasts) of Shawwal, it would be as if he fasted perpetually."
(Muslim)

I am *Grateful* for...
_____
_____

GOALS

Act of Kindness

Smile!	Make Dua
Sadaqah	Spend Time with Family
Read Qur'an	Be Helpful

Healthy Habits

WATER:

EXERCISE: _ _ _ _ _ _ _ _ _ _

MOOD:

Qur'an TRACKER

VERSE: ☐   SURAH: ☐   JUZ': ☐

Reflections

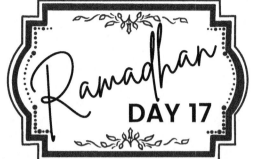

Ramadhan
DAY 17

DAY ☐   **DATE/YEAR**
M/T/W/T/F/S/S

MEAL PLAN

SUHOOR:

IFTAR:

Prayers

SALAT		ON TIME
Maghrib	Sunnah	☐
Isha	Sunnah	☐
Fajr	Sunnah	☐
Dhuhr	Sunnah	☐
Asr	Sunnah	☐
Taraweeh		
Qiyam		

Hadeeth of The Day

Hadhrat Abu Hurairah narrates that The Prophet Muhammad PBUH said:
"Every person has a zakaat (to pay) and the zakaat of the body is fasting."
(Ibn Majah)

I am *Grateful* for...
_____
_____

GOALS

Healthy Habits

WATER:

EXERCISE: _ _ _ _ _ _ _ _ _ _

MOOD:

Act of Kindness

Smile!	Make Dua
Sadaqah	Spend Time with Family
Read Qur'an	Be Helpful

Qur'an TRACKER

VERSE: ☐   SURAH: ☐   JUZ': ☐

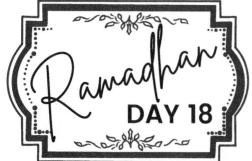

DAY ☐ **DATE/YEAR**
M/T/W/T/F/S/S

[ ]

MEAL PLAN

SUHOOR:

IFTAR:

Prayers

SALAT		ON TIME
Maghrib	Sunnah	☐
Isha	Sunnah	☐
Fajr	Sunnah	☐
Dhuhr	Sunnah	☐
Asr	Sunnah	☐
Taraweeh		
Qiyam		

Hadeeth of The Day

Hadhrat Ibn 'Umar reported that the Apostle of Allah PBUH used to observe i'tikaf (the act of staying in the mosque and devotes oneself to 'ibaadah) in the last ten days of Ramadhan.

(Muslim)

I am *Grateful* for...

_____

_____

GOALS

Act of Kindness

Smile!	Make Dua
Sadaqah	Spend Time with Family
Read Qur'an	Be Helpful

Healthy Habits

WATER:

EXERCISE: _ _ _ _ _ _ _ _ _ _ _

MOOD: 😀 😴 🙁 😠

Qur'an TRACKER

VERSE: [ ]   **SURAH:** [ ]   **JUZ':** [ ]

Reflections

Ramadhan
DAY 19

DAY ☐ DATE/YEAR M/T/W/T/F/S/S ☐

MEAL PLAN

SUHOOR: _____

IFTAR: _____

---

prayers

SALAT		ON TIME
Maghrib	Sunnah	☐
Isha	Sunnah	☐
Fajr	Sunnah	☐
Dhuhr	Sunnah	☐
Asr	Sunnah	☐
Taraweeh		
Qiyam		

HADEETH OF THE DAY

Hadhrat 'Aishah reported that when the last ten nights began Allah's Messenger PBUH kept awake at night (for prayer and devotion), awakened his family, and prepared himself to observe prayer (with more vigour).
(Muslim)

I am *Grateful* for...

_____

_____

GOALS

_____

_____

Act of Kindness

Smile!	Make Dua
Sadaqah	Spend Time with Family
Read Qur'an	Be Helpful

HEALTHY HABITS

WATER: ☐☐☐☐☐☐☐☐

EXERCISE: _ _ _ _ _ _ _ _ _

MOOD: 😀 😴 😢 😠

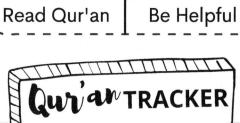

Qur'an TRACKER

VERSE: _____ SURAH: _____ JUZ': _____

Reflections

A Perfect Home

The structure of fasting which may be termed as Shari'ee fasts consist of 3 things namely abstention from eating, drinking and fulfilling one's sexual desires with the Niyyat of fasting. We should ponder a little whether we actually make the Niyyat of Fasting or not.

When a person gets up at the time of Suhoor, then he has the Niyyat of fasting else he wouldn't be awakening to eat at that time of the morning. However, one should be conscious that he is fulfilling the command of Allah then only will servitude enter a person. The pantry, fridge, freezer is filled with food and there is no need to stay hungry but we will fast as it is the command Allah whether it makes sense or not. This is true Abdiyyat (servitude).

Some people are of the opinion that what is the need to remain hungry when there is so much of food available. Those who do not have food should remain hungry. No! Our intention is to fulfill Allah's command. This is when servitude will enter a person. Thus, a person is required to be humble. The thought of "I am the one" should be completely removed from a person.

Total Annihilation is Required

Everyone loves when you negate yourself. If humbleness is in you, everyone will love you, not only does Allah love a humble person but people love a humble person as well. Those that claim that they have achievements to their credit, then people tend to stay away from such a person. You don't want to be close to that person nor do you want to be associated with that person, as he is constantly arrogant and boastful. Such a person is disliked by people and by Allah.

Allah loves a person that negates everything and this is acquired by fasting. When the Nafs and desires are destroyed, the fast is kept properly, then you become the beloved of Allah.

If we only get the taste of Ramadhan it is more enjoyable than the business of December, or a beautiful mansion, or the first night of marriage. This is when our fasts will be profitable, then a person will sincerely desire that the entire year will be Ramadhan. May Allah bless us with that, that is why we are here in the Khanqah and this is what we are striving to achieve. We can in turn then go to our places and show others how to enjoy Ramadhan as well, and let the Ummat know what a bounty Ramadhan is. May Allah bless us with the reality and let us go with these treasures of our Deen.

DAY ☐ **DATE/YEAR** M/T/W/T/F/S/S ☐

MEAL PLAN
- **SUHOOR:**
- **IFTAR:**

Prayers

SALAT		ON TIME
Maghrib	Sunnah	☐
Isha	Sunnah	☐
Fajr	Sunnah	☐
Dhuhr	Sunnah	☐
Asr	Sunnah	☐
Taraweeh		
Qiyam		

Hadeeth of the Day

Hadhrat Abu Hurairah narrated The Prophet Muhamad PBUH as saying: "Fasting is a shield."

(Muslim)

I am Grateful for...
_____
_____

GOALS

Act of Kindness

Smile!	Make Dua
Sadaqah	Spend Time with Family
Read Qur'an	Be Helpful

Healthy Habits

WATER:

EXERCISE: _ _ _ _ _ _ _ _ _ _ _

MOOD:

Qur'an Tracker

VERSE: ☐   **SURAH:** ☐   **JUZ':** ☐

Reflections

Ramadhan DAY 21

DAY ☐ **DATE/YEAR**
M/T/W/T/F/S/S

☐ (box)

MEAL PLAN

SUHOOR:

IFTAR:

Prayers

SALAT		ON TIME
Maghrib	Sunnah	☐
Isha	Sunnah	☐
Fajr	Sunnah	☐
Dhuhr	Sunnah	☐
Asr	Sunnah	☐
Taraweeh		
Qiyam		

Hadeeth of the Day

Hadhrat Abu Hurairah narrated: Allah's Apostle PBUH said: "When the month of Ramadhan starts, the gates of the heaven are opened and the gates of Hell are closed and the devils are chained."
(Bukhari)

I am Grateful for...
_____
_____

GOALS

Act of Kindness

Smile!	Make Dua
Sadaqah	Spend Time with Family
Read Qur'an	Be Helpful

Healthy Habits

WATER: ☐☐☐☐☐☐☐☐

EXERCISE: _ _ _ _ _ _ _ _ _ _

MOOD: 😀 😴 😢 😠

Qur'an TRACKER

VERSE:	SURAH:	JUZ':

Reflections

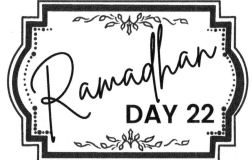

DAY ☐

DATE/YEAR
M/T/W/T/F/S/S

☐

MEAL PLAN

SUHOOR:

IFTAR:

Prayers

SALAT		ON TIME
Maghrib	Sunnah	☐
Isha	Sunnah	☐
Fajr	Sunnah	☐
Dhuhr	Sunnah	☐
Asr	Sunnah	☐
Taraweeh		
Qiyam		

Hadeeth of the Day

Hadhrat Abu Hurairah narrated that The Prophet PBUH said: "Whoever does not give up forged speech and evil actions, Allah is not in need of his leaving his food and drink (i.e. Allah will not accept his fasting)."
(Bukhari)

I am *Grateful* for...
_____
_____

GOALS

Act of Kindness

Smile!	Make Dua
Sadaqah	Spend Time with Family
Read Qur'an	Be Helpful

Healthy Habits

WATER:

EXERCISE: _ _ _ _ _ _ _ _ _ _ _

MOOD:

Qur'an TRACKER

VERSE: ☐   **SURAH:** ☐   **JUZ':** ☐

Reflections

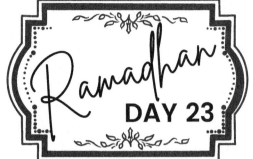

DAY 23

DAY [ ]

DATE/YEAR
M/T/W/T/F/S/S

[ ]

MEAL PLAN

SUHOOR:

IFTAR:

prayers

SALAT		ON TIME
Maghrib	Sunnah	[ ]
Isha	Sunnah	[ ]
Fajr	Sunnah	[ ]
Dhuhr	Sunnah	[ ]
Asr	Sunnah	[ ]
Taraweeh		
Qiyam		

Hadeeth of the Day

Hadhrat Sahl bin Sa'ad narrated:
Allah's Apostle PBUH said:
"The people will remain on the right path as long as they hasten the breaking of the fast."

(Bukhari)

I am *Grateful* for...
_____
_____

GOALS

Act of Kindness

Smile!	Make Dua
Sadaqah	Spend Time with Family
Read Qur'an	Be Helpful

Healthy Habits

WATER:

EXERCISE: _ _ _ _ _ _ _ _ _

MOOD:

Qur'an Tracker

VERSE: [ ]   SURAH: [ ]   JUZ': [ ]

Reflections

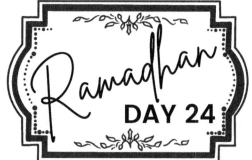

Ramadhan
DAY 24

DAY ☐ DATE/YEAR M/T/W/T/F/S/S ☐

MEAL PLAN
SUHOOR:
IFTAR:

prayers

SALAT		ON TIME
Maghrib	Sunnah	☐
Isha	Sunnah	☐
Fajr	Sunnah	☐
Dhuhr	Sunnah	☐
Asr	Sunnah	☐
Taraweeh		
Qiyam		

Hadeeth of The Day

Hadhrat Abu Hurairah narrates that The Prophet Muhammad PBUH said: "Whoever stands in prayer and 'ibaadah on the night of Power (Laila-tul Qadr) with sincere faith and with sincere hope of gaining reward, his previous sins are forgiven".
(Bukhari and Muslim)

I am *Grateful* for...
_____
_____

GOALS

Act of Kindness

Smile!	Make Dua
Sadaqah	Spend Time with Family
Read Qur'an	Be Helpful

Healthy Habits

WATER: ☐☐☐☐☐☐☐☐

EXERCISE: _ _ _ _ _ _ _ _ _ _

MOOD: 😄 😴 😞 😠

Qur'an TRACKER

VERSE: ☐ SURAH: ☐ JUZ': ☐

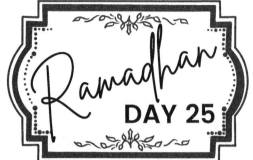

DAY ☐ **DATE/YEAR** M/T/W/T/F/S/S ☐

MEAL PLAN
SUHOOR:

IFTAR:

prayers

SALAT		ON TIME
Maghrib	Sunnah	☐
Isha	Sunnah	☐
Fajr	Sunnah	☐
Dhuhr	Sunnah	☐
Asr	Sunnah	☐
Taraweeh		
Qiyam		

Hadeeth of the Day

Hadhrat 'Aishah reports: "O Messenger of Allah, when I find myself in Laila-tul Qadr, what shall I say?"
The prophet PBUH replied, "Say O Allah Thou art One who pardons. Thou lovest to pardon, so grant me forgiveness."
(Ahmad, Ibn Majah and Tirmizhi)

I am *Grateful* for...
_____
_____

GOALS

Act of Kindness

Smile!	Make Dua
Sadaqah	Spend Time with Family
Read Qur'an	Be Helpful

Healthy Habits

WATER: ☐☐☐☐☐☐☐☐

EXERCISE: _____

MOOD: 😀 😴 😢 😠

Qur'an TRACKER

VERSE: ☐   **SURAH:** ☐   **JUZ':** ☐

Reflections

DAY ☐ **DATE/YEAR**
M/T/W/T/F/S/S

☐

MEAL PLAN

SUHOOR:

IFTAR:

prayers

SALAT		**ON TIME**
Maghrib	Sunnah	☐
Isha	Sunnah	☐
Fajr	Sunnah	☐
Dhuhr	Sunnah	☐
Asr	Sunnah	☐
Taraweeh		
Qiyam		

HaDeeTH of THe DaY

Hadhrat Mu'adh ibn Zuhrah narrated:
The Prophet of Allah PBUH used to say when he broke his fast:
"O Allah, for Thee I have fasted, and with Thy provision I have broken my fast."

(Abu Dawood)

I am *Grateful* for...

_____
_____

GOALS

Act of Kindness

Smile!	Make Dua
Sadaqah	Spend Time with Family
Read Qur'an	Be Helpful

HeaLTHY HaBiTS

WATER:

EXERCISE: _ _ _ _ _ _ _ _ _ _ _

MOOD:

Qur'an TRACKER

VERSE: ☐   **SURAH:** ☐   **JUZ':** ☐

Reflections

DAY ☐ **DATE/YEAR** M/T/W/T/F/S/S

MEAL PLAN

SUHOOR: _____

IFTAR: _____

Prayers

SALAT		ON TIME
Maghrib	Sunnah	☐
Isha	Sunnah	☐
Fajr	Sunnah	☐
Dhuhr	Sunnah	☐
Asr	Sunnah	☐
Taraweeh		
Qiyam		

Hadeeth of The Day

Hadhrat Salman ibn Amir narrated:
The Prophet PBUH said:
"When one of you is fasting, he should break his fast with dates; but if he cannot get any, then (he should break his fast) with water, for water is purifying."

(Abu Dawood)

I am *Grateful* for...

_____
_____

GOALS

Act of Kindness

Smile!	Make Dua
Sadaqah	Spend Time with Family
Read Qur'an	Be Helpful

Healthy Habits

WATER: ☐☐☐☐☐☐☐☐

EXERCISE: _____

MOOD: 😀 😴 😟 😠

Qur'an TRACKER

VERSE: _____ SURAH: _____ JUZ': _____

Reflections

DAY ☐

DATE/YEAR
M/T/W/T/F/S/S

MEAL PLAN

SUHOOR:

IFTAR:

Prayers

SALAT		ON TIME
Maghrib	Sunnah	☐
Isha	Sunnah	☐
Fajr	Sunnah	☐
Dhuhr	Sunnah	☐
Asr	Sunnah	☐
Taraweeh		
Qiyam		

Hadeeth of The Day

Hadhrat Anas ibn Malik narrated:
"The Apostle of Allah PBUH used to break his fast before praying with some fresh dates; but if there were no fresh dates, he had a few dry dates, and if there were no dry dates, he took some mouthfuls of water."
(Abu Dawood)

I am Grateful for...

_____
_____

GOALS

Act of Kindness

Smile!	Make Dua
Sadaqah	Spend Time with Family
Read Qur'an	Be Helpful

Healthy Habits

WATER:

EXERCISE: _ _ _ _ _ _ _ _ _ _ _

MOOD: 😀 😴 🙁 😠

Qur'an TRACKER

VERSE: ☐   SURAH: ☐   JUZ': ☐

Reflections

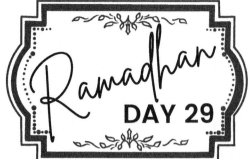

DAY ☐   **DATE/YEAR**
M/T/W/T/F/S/S

MEAL PLAN

SUHOOR:

IFTAR:

---

prayers

SALAT		ON TIME
Maghrib	Sunnah	☐
Isha	Sunnah	☐
Fajr	Sunnah	☐
Dhuhr	Sunnah	☐
Asr	Sunnah	☐
Taraweeh		
Qiyam		

HaDeeTh of The Day

Hadhrat Ibn `Umar reported that
the Messenger of Allah PBUH ordered that
the Sadaqat-ul-Fitr (an obligatory charity
paid at the end of Ramadhan)
should be paid before the people go out
for prayer.
(Bukhari and Muslim)

I am *Grateful* for...
_____
_____

GOALS

HeaLThY HaBiTS

WATER:

EXERCISE: _ _ _ _ _ _ _ _ _ _ _

MOOD: 😀 😴 😢 😠

Act of Kindness

Smile!	Make Dua
Sadaqah	Spend Time with Family
Read Qur'an	Be Helpful

Qur'an TRACKER

VERSE: ____   **SURAH:** ____   **JUZ':** ____

Reflections

Ramadhan DAY 30

DAY ☐ **DATE/YEAR** M/T/W/T/F/S/S ☐

MEAL PLAN
- SUHOOR:
- IFTAR:

prayers

SALAT		ON TIME
Maghrib	Sunnah	☐
Isha	Sunnah	☐
Fajr	Sunnah	☐
Dhuhr	Sunnah	☐
Asr	Sunnah	☐
Taraweeh		
Qiyam		

Hadeeth of the Day

Hadhrat Muaz Bin Jabal reported that The Prophet PBUH said to him:
"Shall I not guide you towards the means of goodness? Fasting is a shield; charity wipes away sin as water extinguishes fire."
(Tirmizhi)

I am Grateful for...
_____
_____

GOALS

Act of Kindness

Smile!	Make Dua
Sadaqah	Spend Time with Family
Read Qur'an	Be Helpful

Healthy Habits

WATER:

EXERCISE: _ _ _ _ _ _ _ _ _ _ _

MOOD:

Qur'an TRACKER

VERSE: [   ]   SURAH: [   ]   JUZ': [   ]

Reflections

Printed in Great Britain
by Amazon

38644230R00037